ROSARY PSALMS

PETER HUYCK

Rosary Psalms

ST PAULS

For the monks of New Melleray Abbey

ST PAULS
Morpeth Terrrace, London SW1P 1EP, UK
Moyglare Road, Maynooth, Co. Kildare, Ireland

© ST PAULS (UK) 1994

ISBN 085439 489 3

First published 1994. Reprinted 1996, 1999

Produced in the EC
Cover: Mary Lou Winters
Set by TuKan, High Wycombe

Printed by Alden Press, Oxford

ST PAULS is an activity of the priests and brothers of the
Society of St Paul who proclaim the Gospel through the media
of social communication

Contents

The Glorious Mysteries

Rosary Prayers

Introduction

The Rosary is an ancient and powerful prayer to Mary, the Mother of God. The *Rosary Psalms* are a meditation for the Rosary based on the Psalms.

The history of the Rosary begins with the widespread mediaeval practice of praying 150 Our Fathers in imitation of the 150 Psalms and counting them on a cord with 50 knots. One of the old counting strings is still preserved which dates back to the year 900. For the laity, praying this prayer (which takes about an hour) was an attempt to share in the spirituality of the monasteries where the Psalms were prayed in choir.

Prayer beads soon appeared. In her will (c. 1075) the Countess Godiva of Coventry left a certain monastery "the circlet of precious stones which she had threaded on a cord in order that by fingering them one after another she might count her prayers exactly." By 1268 there were four recognized trade guilds in the city of Paris alone which made prayer beads.

The popularity in the 11th century of the Little Office of the Blessed Virgin Mary (which was, of course, itself based on the Psalms) gave rise to the Hail Mary as a popular prayer in its own right. The words of Gabriel ("Hail, full of grace, the Lord is with thee, blessed art thou among women", cf. Luke 1:28) and the words of Elizabeth ("Blessed art thou among women and blessed is the fruit of thy womb," cf. Luke 1:41) frequently appear as the versicle and responsory in the Office. The power of prayer to Mary was grafted onto the beads when people began reciting 150 Hail Marys in imitation of the prayer of 150 Our Fathers. The Hail Mary as then prayed was simply:

> Hail Mary, full of grace, the Lord is with thee. Blessed art thou among women and blessed is the fruit of thy womb.

In the 13th and 14th centuries there was a number of attempts to make the prophecies of the Psalms more explicit with regard to the lives of Jesus and Mary. These were the so-called psalters of Jesus and Mary. Here is an example of the first "psalm" from one such "psalter" of Mary. It is 13th century, consists of 150 quatrains, and was attributed to Archbishop Stephen Langton:

> Hail, Virgin of Virgins, mother without peer,
> Worthy without seed of man to bear a child,
> Make us often to meditate upon the law of
>   the Lord

And come to beatitude in the glory of the
kingdom.

Meditation on the law of the Lord is the concept
which links this quatrain with Psalm One. Some of
the later of these Psalters were composed with less
conformity to the Psalms and became in many
cases mere accounts of the life of Jesus or Mary
told in 150 short phrases.

These popular Psalters influenced the trend in
the 15th century of adding a meditation to each
Hail Mary in the prayer of 150 Hail Marys.
Meditations were first added to 50 Hail Marys in
this fashion by Dominic of Prussia, a Carthusian
monk, who lived from 1384-1460. Here is
Dominic's first meditation:

Hail Mary, full of grace, the Lord is with thee.
Blessed art thou amongst women, and blessed
is the fruit of thy womb, Jesus Christ, whom
thou didst conceive by the Holy Spirit, through
the message of the angel. Amen.

When the innovation appeared of interspersing
15 Our Fathers between the 150 Hail Marys (thus
creating the decades), meditations were added to
the Our Fathers as well. The result was 165
meditations in all. By the time this happened,

printing had been invented. Here is the first decade as it appeared in the *Rosary of the Glorious Virgin Mary* by Alberto da Castello OP in 1521.

The Joyful Rosary

The Our Father Mystery: Mary, the Virgin, has conceived Jesus. The longing of the holy patriarchs who prayed for the incarnation of Christ.

1. Mary was prefigured through types in the Old Testament.
2. The Virgin Mary was foretold by the holy prophets.
3 The birth of the Virgin Mary was foretold by an angel.
4. The Virgin Mary was sanctified in the womb of St Anne.
5. The birth of the glorious Virgin Mary.
6. Mary is presented in the Temple.
7. The holy life of Mary in the Temple.
8. Mary is betrothed to Joseph by the High Priest.
9. The Virgin Mary is chosen by God to be his mother.
10. The angel announces to Mary the message of the Incarnation.

The Rosary as we know it today resulted from these Hail Mary meditations slowly disappearing and the Our Father meditations remaining and becoming our familiar mysteries.

The meditation in this book resembles the 165 point meditations of the early 16th century but with two important differences, both of which are characteristic of Scriptural Rosaries. First, it reaches back beyond the paraphrases of the Psalms into the Scriptures themselves for the meditations. Second, the meditations for each Hail Mary are all focused directly on the mystery, which is the old Our Father meditation.

Pope Pius XII likens picking up the Rosary to picking up young David's sling. Since this meditation is drawn entirely from the Psalms, many of which were attributed to David, when you pick it up it is like picking up both David's sling and David's harp. Use this meditation occasionally to enrich your own imaginative meditations on the mysteries of the Rosary (it isn't too long to memorize). It can also be used for group recitation of the Rosary. Read the passage in **bold** type before each Our Father, and the subsequent passages before each Hail Mary.

When the Rosary was indulgenced by St Pius V in 1569, it consisted of 150 Hail Marys, 15 Our Fathers, and meditation on the mysteries. Praying a third of the Rosary was also indulgenced. The Rosary is still indulgenced today, and the structure is still the same as it was in 1569 (*Enchiridion of Indulgences*, 1969, pp. 67-68).

In the Apostolic Exhortation *Marialis Cultus* (2 February 1974), Pope Paul VI observes that "by its nature the recitation of the Rosary calls for a quiet rhythm and a lingering pace, helping the individual to meditate on the mysteries of the Lord's life as seen through the eyes of her who was closest to the Lord. In this way the unfathomable riches of these mysteries are unfolded" (§47). He goes on to say that "we desire… to recommend that this very worthy devotion should not be propagated in a way that is too one-sided or exclusive. The Rosary is an excellent prayer, but the faithful should feel serenely free in its regard. They should be drawn to its calm recitation by its intrinsic appeal" (§55).

The Rosary is like an ancient fountain from which pure water still flows. Try it. Ask Mary for some favour, then work your way through the meditation on the beads. See what happens.

Reading the Psalms

The language of the Psalms is the language of poetry and prophecy. These deep prophecies have been studied for centuries. Try to imagine, for example, that these words

> Deep is calling on deep,
> in the roar of waters.   (Psalm 41:8)

might foreshadow this event:

> In the sixth month the angel
> Gabriel was sent by God to a
> town in Galilee called Nazareth,
> to a virgin engaged to a man whose name
> was Joseph, of the house of David.
> The virgin's name was Mary.
>   (Luke 1:26-27)

Try to hear the echo of these words from the Psalms,

> Listen, O daughter, give ear to my words:
> forget your own people and your father's
> house.   (Psalm 44:11)

in these words of Gabriel:

> Greetings, favoured one!
> The Lord is with you.   (Luke 1:28)

> Blessed are you among women.   (Luke 1:42)

Compare this prophecy from the Psalms,

> I will never lie to David.
> His dynasty shall last for ever.
>   (Psalm 88:36-37)

to this prophecy of Gabriel:

> The Lord God will give to him the throne
> of his ancestor David. He will reign over
> the house of Jacob forever,
> and of his kingdom there will be no end.
>   (Luke 1:32-33)

When Mary responds to Elizabeth's greetings, she says,

> My soul magnifies the Lord,
> and my spirit rejoices in God my Saviour.
>   (Luke 1:47)

while a similar passage in the Psalms reads:

> My soul, give thanks to the Lord,
> all my being, bless his holy name.
>
> (Psalm 102:1)

Imagine the thoughts of God on the night that Jesus was born,

> You are my Son. (Psalm 2:7)

and the thoughts of Christ:

> It was you who created my being,
> knit me together in my mother's womb.
>
> (Psalm 138:13)

Look for these words of the aged Simeon,

> Master, now you are dismissing
> your servant in peace,
> according to your word;
> for my eyes have seen your salvation,
> which you have prepared in the presence of
>   all peoples. (Luke 2:29-31)

The
Joyful Mysteries

I

The annunciation of the Archangel Gabriel to the Virgin Mary

I rejoiced to do your will as though all riches were mine.

118:14

Deep is calling on deep,
in the roar of waters.   41:8

Listen, O daughter, give ear to my words: 44:11

Forget your own people and your
      father's house.   44:11

So will the king desire your beauty: 44:12

He is your lord, pay homage to him.   44:12

I will never lie to David.
His dynasty shall last for ever.   88:36-37

In my sight his throne is like the sun.   88:37

Like the moon, it shall endure for ever,
a faithful witness in the skies.   88:38

The Lord does whatever he wills,
in heaven, on earth, in the seas.   134:6

I have said to the Lord: "You are my God."
                                                                  139:7

II

The visitation of the Virgin Mary to the parents of John the Baptist

**My heart is ready, O God,
my heart is ready.**

56:8

My soul, give thanks to the Lord,
all my being, bless his holy name. 102:1

He has never despised
nor scorned the poverty of the poor. 21:25

Holy his name, to be feared. 110:9

As the heavens are high above the earth
so strong is his love for those who fear him.
102:11

Yours is a mighty arm, O Lord;
your hand is strong, your right hand ready. 88:14

He pours contempt upon princes,
makes them wander in trackless wastes. 106:40

He raises the needy from distress. 106:41

He fills the hungry with good things. 106:9

He has remembered his truth and love
for the house of Israel. 97:3

He remembered his holy word,
which he gave to Abraham his servant. 104:42

III

The birth of Jesus in Bethlehem

You are my Son.
2:7

You are my Son.
It is I who have begotten you this day.   2:7

Ask and I shall bequeath you the nations,
put the ends of the earth in your possession.   2:8

It was you who created my being,
knit me together in my mother's womb.   138:13

I thank you for the wonder of my being.   138:14

Already you knew my soul
when I was being fashioned in secret
and moulded in the depths of the earth. 138:14-15

Your eyes saw all my actions,
they were all of them written in your book. 138:16

Every one of my days was decreed
before one of them came into being.   138:16

The kings of Tarshish and the sea coasts
shall pay him tribute.
The kings of Sheba and Seba
shall bring him gifts.   71:10

Before him all kings shall fall prostrate,
all nations shall serve him.   71:11

For he shall save the poor when they cry
and the needy who are helpless.   71:12

IV

The presentation of Jesus in the Temple

**You do not ask for holocaust and victim.
Instead, here am I.**

39:7-8

They did his will; they kept the law,
which he, the Lord, had given.   98:7

I rejoiced when I heard them say:
"Let us go to God's house."   121:1

Now our feet are standing
within your gates, O Jerusalem.   121:2

Jerusalem! The mountains surround her,
so the Lord surrounds his people
both now and for ever.   124:2

* * *

They are happy, who dwell in your house,
for ever singing your praise.   83:5

Remember your word to your servant
by which you gave me hope.   118:49

When can I enter and see
the face of God?   41:3

All the ends of the earth have seen
the salvation of our God!   97:3

There David's stock will flower.   131:17

He has remembered his truth and love
for the house of Israel.   97:3

V

The finding of Jesus in the Temple

I burn with zeal for your house.

68:10

Jerusalem is built as a city
strongly compact.
It is there that the tribes go up,
the tribes of the Lord.   121:3-4

For Israel's law it is,
there to praise the Lord's name.   121:4

I am like a growing olive tree
in the house of God.   51:10

How lovely is your dwelling place,
Lord, God of hosts.   83:2

One day within your courts
is better than a thousand elsewhere.   83:11

       * * *

I am wearied with all my crying,
my throat is parched.   68:4

My eyes are wasted away
from looking for my God.   68:4

I have become like a pelican in the wilderness,
like an owl in desolate places.   101:7

I lie awake and I moan
like some lonely bird on a roof.   101:8

My soul is longing for the Lord
more than watchman for daybreak.   129:6

The
Sorrowful Mysteries

VI

The agony of Jesus in the Garden of Gethsemane

Call on me in the day of distress.
49:15

In my anguish I called to the Lord;
I cried to my God for help.   17:7

Fear is all around me,
as they plot together against me,
as they plan to take my life.   30:14

My heart is stricken within me,
death's terror is on me.   54:5

Trembling and fear fall upon me
and horror overwhelms me.   54:6

In God I trust, I shall not fear:
what can mortal man do to me?   55:5

You are my father, my God,
the rock who saves me.   88:27

You are my father, my God,
the rock who saves me.   88:27

You are my father, my God,
the rock who saves me.   88:27

You are my refuge,
all I have in the land of the living.   141:6

Now, Lord, what is there to wait for?
In you rests all my hope.   38:8

VII

The scourging of Jesus at the pillar

They ploughed my back like ploughmen, drawing long furrows.

128:3

Examine me, Lord, and try me;
O test my heart and my mind.   25:2

I was silent, not opening my lips,
because this was all your doing.   38:10

Take away your scourge from me.   38:11

I am crushed by the blows of your hand.   38:11

You punish man's sins and correct him;
like the moth you devour all the treasures.   38:12

Mortal man is no more than a breath;
O Lord, hear my prayer.   38:12-13

In your house I am a passing guest,
a pilgrim, like all my ancestors.   38:13

Look away that I may breathe again
before I depart and am no more.   38:14

You, O God, have tested us,
you have tried us as silver is tried.   65:10

O give your strength to your servant
and save your handmaid's son.   85:16

VIII

The crowning of Jesus with thorns

My foes encircle me with deadly intent.
16:9

Their hearts tight shut, their mouths speak
    proudly.   16:10

They advance against me, and now they
    surround me.   16:11

Now that I am in trouble they gather,
they gather and mock me.   34:15

They take me by surprise and strike me
and tear me to pieces.   34:15

They provoke me with mockery on mockery
and gnash their teeth.   34:16

O Lord, how long will you look on?   34:17

Come to my rescue!   34:17

Save my life from these raging beasts,
my soul from these lions.   34:17

Do not let my lying foes
rejoice over me.   34:19

Do not let those who hate me unjustly
wink eyes at each other.   34:19

IX

The carrying of the cross by Jesus to Calvary

**They go out, they go out, full of tears,
carrying seed for the sowing.**

125:6

May my footsteps be firm to obey your statutes.	118:5

I am a pilgrim on earth;
show me your commands. 118:19

I will run the way of your commands;
you give freedom to my heart. 118:32

Guide me in the path of your commands;
for there is my delight. 118:35

Your commands have been my delight;
these I have loved. 118:47

It was good for me to be afflicted,
to learn your statutes. 118:71

Your word is a lamp for my steps
and a light for my path. 118:105

Your will is my heritage for ever,
the joy of my heart. 118:111

Long have I known that your will
is established for ever. 118:152

Though my foes and oppressors are countless
I have not swerved from your will. 118:157

X

The crucifixion and death of Jesus

O God, they have set your sanctuary on fire: they have razed and profaned the place where you dwell.

73:7

My God, my God, why have you forsaken me?
You are far from my plea and the cry of my
    distress.   21:2

O my God, I call by day and you give no reply;
I call by night and I find no peace.   21:3

All who see me deride me.
They curl their lips, they toss their heads.   21:8

"He trusted in the Lord, let him save him;
let him release him if this is his friend."   21:9

Like water I am poured out,
disjointed are all my bones.
My heart has become like wax,
it is melted within my breast.   21:15

Parched as burnt clay is my throat,
my tongue cleaves to my jaws.   21:16

They tear holes in my hands and my feet
and lay me in the dust of death.   21:17

I can count every one of my bones.   21:18

These people stare at me and gloat;
they divide my clothing among them.
They cast lots for my robe.   21:18-19

Into your hands I commend my spirit.   30:6

The
Glorious Mysteries

XI

The resurrection of Jesus from the dead

The foe is destroyed, eternally ruined.
9:7

"For the poor who are oppressed and
    the needy who groan
I myself will arise," says the Lord.   11:6

"I will grant them the salvation for
    which they thirst."   11:6

From on high he reached down and seized me;
he drew me forth from the mighty waters.
He snatched me from my powerful foe.   17:17-18

He brought me forth into freedom,
he saved me because he loved me.   17:20

I am sure now that the Lord
will give victory to his anointed.   19:7

O Lord, you have raised my soul from the dead,
restored me to life from those who sink into
    the grave.   29:4

At night there are tears, but joy comes with dawn.
                   29:6

I will make him my first-born,
the highest of the kings of the earth.   88:28

I will keep my love for him always;
with him my covenant shall last.   88:29

I will establish his dynasty for ever,
make his throne endure as the heavens.   88:30

XII

The ascension of Jesus into heaven

**O gates, lift high your heads;
grow higher, ancient doors.
Let him enter, the king of glory!**

23:7

It is I who have begotten you this day. 2:7

Ask and I shall bequeath you the nations,
put the ends of the earth in your possession. 2:8

Sit on my right:
your foes I will put beneath your feet. 109:1

A prince from the day of your birth
on the holy mountains. 109:3

From the womb before daybreak
I begot you. 109:3

You are a priest for ever,
a priest like Melchizedek of old. 109:4

The stone which the builders rejected
has become the corner stone. 117:22

This is the work of the Lord,
a marvel in our eyes. 117:23

This day was made by the Lord;
we rejoice and are glad. 117:24

O gates, lift high your heads;
grow higher, ancient doors.
Let him enter, the king of glory! 23:9

XIII

*The descent of the Holy Spirit
upon the apostles*

**He sends out his word to the earth
and swiftly runs his command.**

147:15

The Lord's voice resounding on the waters,
the Lord on the immensity of waters.   28:3

The voice of the Lord, full of power,
the voice of the Lord, full of splendour.   28:4

The Lord's voice flashes flames of fire.   28:7

The God of glory thunders.
In his temple they all cry: "Glory!"   28:9-10

They feast on the riches of your house;
they drink from the stream of your delight.   35:9

In you is the source of life
and in your light we see light.   35:10

O send forth your light and your truth;
let these be my guide.   42:3

Let them bring me to your holy mountain,
to the place where you dwell.   42:3

I will come to the altar of God,
the God of my joy.   42:4

You send forth your spirit, they are created;
and you renew the face of the earth.   103:30

XIV

The assumption of the Virgin Mary into heaven

**Of you my heart has spoken:
"Seek his face."**

26:8

My heart rejoices, my soul is glad;
even my body shall rest in safety.   15:9

You will not leave my soul among the dead,
nor let your beloved know decay.   15:10

You will show me the path of life,
the fullness of joy in your presence.   15:11

From on high he reached down and seized me;
he drew me forth from the mighty waters.   17:17

O precious in the eyes of the Lord
is the death of his faithful.   115:15

Our life, like a bird, has escaped
from the snare of the fowler.   123:7

Indeed the snare has been broken
and we have escaped.   123:7

You stretch out your hand and save me.   137:7

Your love, O Lord, is eternal,
discard not the work of your hands.   137:8

Discard not the work of your hands.   137:8

XV

The coronation of the Blessed Virgin Mary as Queen of heaven and earth

**He fixes the number of the stars;
he calls each one by its name.**

146:4

I through the greatness of your love
have access to your house. 5:8

I bow down before your holy temple,
filled with awe. 5:8

O Lord, it is you who are my portion and cup;
it is you yourself who are my prize. 15:5

The lot marked out for me is my delight:
welcome indeed the heritage that falls to me! 15:6

You are the fairest of the children of men
and graciousness is poured upon your lips:
because God has blessed you for evermore. 44:3

From the ivory palace you are greeted
with music. 44:9

The daughter of the king is clothed with
splendour,
her robes embroidered with pearls set in gold.
44:14

She is led to the king with her maiden
companions.
They are escorted amid gladness and joy;
they pass within the palace of the king. 44:15

→

←

Sons shall be yours in place of your fathers:
you will make them princes over all the earth.

44:17

May this song make your name for ever
    remembered.
May the peoples praise you from age to age.

44:18

Rosary Prayers

The Our Father

Our Father,
who art in heaven,
hallowed be thy name;
thy kingdom come,
thy will be done on earth as it is in heaven.
Give us this day our daily bread;
and forgive us our trespasses
as we forgive those who trespass against us;
and lead us not into temptation,
but deliver us from evil. Amen

◆

The Hail Mary

Hail Mary, full of grace,
the Lord is with thee.
Blessed art thou among women,
and blessed is the fruit of thy womb, Jesus.
Holy Mary, Mother of God,
pray for us sinners,
now and at the hour of our death. Amen.

The Glory Be

Glory be to the Father,
    and to the Son,
    and to the Holy Spirit.
As it was in the beginning,
    is now, and ever shall be,
    world without end. Amen.

◆

The Hail, Holy Queen

Hail, holy Queen, Mother of mercy;
    hail, our life, our sweetness, and our hope.
To you do we cry, poor banished children of Eve.
To you do we send up our sighs,
    mourning and weeping in this valley of tears.
Turn then, most gracious advocate,
    your eyes of mercy towards us,
    and after this our exile,
    show unto us the blessed fruit of your womb,
        Jesus.
O clement, O loving, O sweet Virgin Mary.

Mary's Song of Praise

My soul magnifies the LORD,
    and my spirit rejoices in God my Saviour,
for he has looked with favour on the lowliness
        of his servant.
Surely, from now on all
    generations will call me blessed;
for the Mighty One has done great things for me,
    and holy is his name.
His mercy is for those who fear him
    from generation to generation.
He has shown strength with his arm;
      he has scattered the proud in the
        thoughts of their hearts.
He has brought down the powerful
      from their thrones,
    and lifted up the lowly;
he has filled the hungry with good things,
    and sent the rich away empty.
He has helped his servant Israel,
    in remembrance of his mercy,
according to the promise he made
      to our ancestors,
    to Abraham and to his descendants forever.

(Luke 1:47-55)

Hannah's Prayer

My heart exults in the LORD;
    my strength is exalted in my God.
My mouth derides my enemies,
    because I rejoice in my victory.

There is no Holy One like the LORD,
    no one besides you;
    there is no Rock like our God.
Talk no more so very proudly,
    let not arrogance come from your mouth;
for the LORD is a God of knowledge,
    and by him actions are weighed.
The bows of the mighty are broken,
    but the feeble gird on strength.
Those who were full have hired
      themselves out for bread,
    but those who were hungry are fat with spoil.
The barren has borne seven,
    but she who has many children is forlorn.
The LORD kills and brings to life;
    he brings down to Sheol and raises up.
The LORD makes poor and makes rich;
    he brings low, he also exalts.
He raises up the poor from the dust;
    he lifts the needy from the ash heap,

to make them sit with princes
    and inherit a seat of honour.
For the pillars of the earth are the Lord's,
    and on them he has set the world.

He will guard the feet of his faithful ones,
    but the wicked shall be cut off in darkness;
    for not by might does one prevail.
The Lord! His adversaries shall be shattered;
    the Most High will thunder in heaven.
The Lord will judge the ends of the earth;
    he will give strength to his king,
    and exalt the power of his anointed.

                (1 Samuel 2:1-10)

The Priestly Benediction

The LORD bless you and keep you;
the LORD make his face to shine upon you,
   and be gracious to you;
The LORD lift up his countenance upon you,
   and give you peace.

(Numbers 6:24-26)

Sources

Leo XIII published encyclicals on the Rosary every year from 1883 to 1898.

Fr Herbert Thurston, a Jesuit priest, published a series of fifteen articles on the history of the Rosary in The Month from 1900 to 1924.

Fr Franz Willam brought out a book entitled *The Rosary: Its History and Meaning* in 1947 on the occasion of the canonization of St Louis-Marie Grignion de Montfort.

St Louis-Marie Grignion de Montfort (1673-1716) wrote *The Secret of the Rosary*, which is the classic on the subject.

Paul VI's Apostolic Exhortation *Marialis Cultus* (2 February 1974) devotes almost the entire third section to the Rosary.

John Gabriel's *Scriptural Rosary* (1961) was the first modern meditation for the Rosary based directly on the Scriptures.

Acknowledgements

The extracts from the Psalms in this publication are taken from THE PSALMS, A New Translation, published by Harper Collins Ltd, used by permission of A.P. Watt Ltd on behalf of The Grail, England. The numbering of the Psalms in this translation differs slightly from other modern translations.

The other Scripture quotations in this publication are from the New Revised Standard Version of the Bible, copyright © 1989 by the Division of Christian Education of the National Council of the Churches of Christ in the USA, and are used by permission.

The Six Chaplet Rosary
Alan Robinson

To the traditional Rosary three further Chaplets are suggested: the Opening Mysteries (Creation and Covenant); the Prophetic Mysteries (the Coming Messiah); and the Continuing Mysteries (the Living Faith). For each decade in all six chaplets a biblical passage, a prayer and themes for meditation are included.   085439 473 7

The Rosary

This little booklet illustrates each Mystery of the Rosary with a quotation from the Gospel and ends each with a short reflection. Illustrated in full colour.   085439 444 3

The Rosary Concertina

The fifteen Mysteries of the Rosary are introduced with an appropriate biblical verse and a bible reading reference, followed by a very short prayer of petition. Each mystery is illustrated.

MM91R